# CONTEnTs

# THE WORLD OF ROBOTS

The face of one of the world's greatest scientists — physicist Albert Einstein — lives on in this robot named Albert Hubo. Albert's brain is a computer and its eyes are cameras, but its realistic skin, humanlike movements and ability to carry on a conversation might just make you forget you're talking to a robot.

There aren't many robots like Albert … yet. But there *are* lots of other robots hard at work in our world. Robots run errands in hospitals and patrol buildings at night. They spray-paint cars and shear sheep. They play soccer and chess. They descend into burbling volcanoes, examine the ocean floor and explore the surface of Mars.

*Albert Hubo*

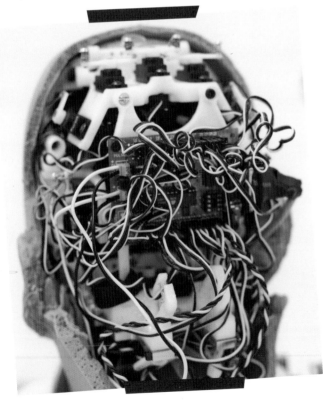

**Albert Hubo's "brain" contains 31 small motors.**

Not long ago, robots were more science fiction than science fact. But today, they are part of our lives, even though we may not know it. And advances in computer science and other technologies are opening new doors for roboticists (people who invent robots). By the time you have grandchildren, robots may be as common as computers — and even more useful.

# ROBOTS

## By the Editors of *YES Mag*

**Kids Can Press**

## Dedication

To the young science keeners who make creating *YES* and *KNOW* magazines a blast.

## Acknowledgments

The author would like to thank her colleagues at *YES* and *KNOW* magazines, Jude Isabella, Shannon Hunt and David Garrison, for their ideas and support, as well as the following people who reviewed the text for accuracy: Robert J. Ambrose, NASA Johnson Space Center; David Calkins, Robotics Society of America; Todd Camill; Ron Diftler, NASA Johnson Space Center; Nora Distefano, Intuitive Surgical, Inc.; Tim Eck; Aaron Edsinger, Human Robotics Group, MIT; Regan Genter, Autonomous Undersea Systems Institute; Alicia Jones, American Honda Motor Co. Inc.; James McLurkin, MIT Computer Science and Artificial Intelligence Laboratory; Pamela Mahoney, Mohr Davidow Ventures; Keith Shepherd, Canadian Scientific Submersible Facility; Julie Simard, Canadian Space Agency; Anissa Agah St. Pierre, Coordinator for Women in Computer Science & Engineering, University of Victoria; Nishio Shuichi, Advanced Telecommunication Research Institute: Intelligent Robotics and Communication; Ron Weaver; Guy Webster, NASA Jet Propulsion Laboratory; and Marie Williams, SHIFT Communications.

The *YES Mag* team member who who worked on this book is Adrienne Mason.

Kids Can Press acknowledges the financial support of the Government of Ontario, through the Ontario Media Development Corporation's Ontario Book Initiative; the Ontario Arts Council; the Canada Council for the Arts; and the Government of Canada, through the BPIDP, for our publishing activity.

| | |
|---|---|
| Published in Canada by Kids Can Press Ltd. 29 Birch Avenue Toronto, ON M4V 1E2 | Published in the U.S. by Kids Can Press Ltd. 2250 Military Road Tonawanda, NY 14150 |

www.kidscanpress.com

Edited by Valerie Wyatt
Designed by Julia Naimska
Illustrations by Howie Woo
Printed and bound in Singapore

The paper used to print this book was produced with elemental chlorine-free pulp, harvested from managed sustainable forests.

The hardcover edition of this book is smyth sewn casebound. The paperback edition of this book is limp sewn with a drawn-on cover.

CM 08 0 9 8 7 6 5 4 3 2 1
CM PA 08 0 9 8 7 6 5 4 3 2 1

## Photo Credits

**Cover** Inozemtcev Konstantin, Shutterstock. **Page 1** courtesy NASA. **Page 4** courtesy Hanson Robotics. **Page 5** upper left and bottom Blue Sky Studios/Twentieth Century Fox Film Corporation; Upper right COURTESY OF LUCASFILM LTD. *Star Wars: Episode IV — A New Hope* © 1977 and 1997 Lucasfilm Ltd. & ™. All rights reserved. Used under authorization. Unauthorized duplication is a violation of applicable law. **Page 8** COURTESY OF LUCASFILM LTD. *Star Wars: Episode IV — A New Hope* © 1977 and 1997 Lucasfilm Ltd. & ™. All rights reserved. Used under authorization. Unauthorized duplication is a violation of applicable law. **Page 9** Sean P. Leach, Shutterstock. **Page 10** Chris Hellyar, Shutterstock. **Page 11** top Wowwee; bottom Carnegie Mellon University. **Page 13** top courtesy Adept Technology, Inc.; bottom courtesy KUKA Schweissanlagen GmbH. **Page 14** courtesy of Northrop Grumman Subsidiary, Remotec Inc. **Page 15** top Erich Rome; bottom Foster-Miller, Inc. **Page 16** FEMA. **Page 17** top and middle Inuktun Services. Ltd.; bottom Courtesy of iRobot Corp. **Pages 18–19** bottom and middle courtesy of Intuitive Surgical, Inc, 2007; upper right Hemera Technologies Inc. **Page 20** upper left AETHON; other photos Robotic Systems & Technologies, Inc. **Page 21** upper THE CANDIAN PRESS/AP/Jeff Chiu; lower THE CANDIAN PRESS/AP/Caleb Jones. **Page 22** Canadian Scientific Submersible Facility. **Page 23** upper Tom Kleindinst, Woods Hole Oceanographic Institution; lower The Autonomous Undersea Systems Institute. **Page 24** NASA/JPL-Caltech. **Page 25** both photos NASA. **Page 26** both photos American Honda Motor Co., Inc. **Page 27** upper Delft University of Technology; lower Garth Zeglin, 1991; right A.Herzog, courtesy Biologically Inspired Robotics Group, EPFL. **Page 28** left Osaka University and Kokoro Co. Ltd.; right ATR Intelligent Robotics and Communication Laboratories. **Page 29** Todd Camill/Entertainment Technology Center/ Carnegie Mellon University. **Pages 30–31** Roomba courtesy of iRobot Corp; pool-cleaning robot courtesy of iRobot Corp; lawn-mowing robot Friendly Robotics; security robot courtesy of Dr. Haipeng Xie and www.drrobot.com; Scooba, courtesy of iRobot Corp; Wakamaru courtesy of Mitsubishi Heavy Industries. **Page 32** all photos RoboGames. **Page 33** upper 2007 *FIRST* LEGO® League World Festival/photo by J.R. Hicks; middle and lower courtesy K-Team/www.k-team.com. **Page 34** upper right Perspective Branding; lower Mack Fraga Designs. **Page 35** upper Wowwee; middle OMRON Corp; lower Dr. Takanori Shibata/AIST. **Page 36** Stanford Racing Team. **Page 37** Inozemtcev Konstantin, Shutterstock. **Page 38** Aaron Edsinger. **Page 39** upper Aaron Edsinger; lower Zach & Kim DeBord. **Pages 40–41** all photos, Peter Menzel/Science Photo Library. **Page 42** left Shutterstock; right Benson Limketkai/SRI International. **Page 43** left Philip Greenspun. **Page 45** iCube Solutions. **Page 46** Chris Harvey Shutterstock.

**Library and Archives Canada Cataloguing in Publication**

Robots : from everyday to out of this world / written by the editors of Yes Mag.

Includes index.
ISBN 978-1-55453-203-2 (bound).
ISBN 978-1-55453-204-9 (pbk.)

1. Robots—Juvenile literature. 2. Androids—Juvenile literature.

TJ211.2.R59 2008   j629.8'92   C2007-906553-8

Kids Can Press is a **corus**™ Entertainment company

# Robots We Know and Love

If these movie star robots are your image of a robot, you're in for a surprise. Very few robots can do the things these stars of the screen do.

*R2-D2 from* Star Wars

*Sonny from* I, Robot

*Rodney, Fender and the gang from* Robots

# From Wooden Cogs to Working Robots

Have you ever wanted a robot that did your chores? Well, you're not alone. For centuries, people have been imagining and inventing robotlike machines to make their lives easier. They've also been tinkering away just for the fun of it. All of that experimenting and inventing has led to bigger and better things — today's robots.

**Late 1400s** Artist and inventor Leonardo da Vinci builds a mechanical lion. He also draws plans for a "robot-knight" run by pulleys, wooden disks and gears.

**1600s** Mechanical puppets called karakuri dolls are built in Japan. Some can serve tea.

**1738** French inventor Jacques de Vaucanson builds a human-sized flute player that plays 12 songs and a mechanical duck that flaps its wings, sits, eats grain and even poops.

**1774** Swiss craftsman Pierre Jacquet-Droz and his son build a mechanical boy that dips a pen into an inkwell and writes short messages.

**Late 1700s – early 1800s** Jacques de Vaucanson and Joseph Jacquard design looms that use holes punched in cards to determine the pattern woven into fabrics. Edmund Cartwright invents a steam-powered loom. From these inventions come automated looms, the world's first factory robots.

**1898** Nikola Tesla demonstrates a remote-controlled, bathtub-sized boat. It is the first-ever ROV (remotely-operated vehicle). Today, many robots are operated by remote control.

**1946** Americans John P. Eckert, Jr. and John Mauchly build the world's first successful computer. ENIAC is the size of a boxcar and uses 18 000 vacuum tubes. It is the great-granddaddy of the tiny computers that will one day control robots.

**1890** American mathematician Herman Hollerith develops a calculator that does math by reading holes in punched cards. These punched cards pave the way for the first computers, an important component of modern robotics.

**1948** Tiny transistors replace big vacuum tubes. Shrinking these and other computer components make it possible to give robots computer "brains."

**1948** William Grey Walter builds the first robot that can make its own decisions. He calls it *Machina speculatrix* (Latin for "the machine that watches"), but everyone else calls it "the tortoise." When its sensors detect light, the tortoise moves toward it.

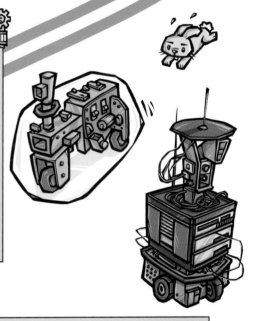

**1954** Americans George Devol and Joseph Engelberger install Unimate, a mechanical arm, in an auto assembly plant. This 1800 kg (4000 lb.) robot changes assembly lines forever.

**1969** Scientists at the Stanford Research Institute in California complete Shakey, a mobile robot that can "think" and respond to the world around it. The wobbly, wheeled robot can locate objects and avoid obstacles in a room. Robots are on the move!

# ROBOTS 101

The robot R2-D2 is possibly the most charming hunk of metal ever to hit the silver screen. This ace mechanic starred in the Star Wars movies and was the laid-back sidekick of C-3PO, a walking, talking, argumentative, glittery gold humanoid.

Real-life robots aren't much like movie star robots. For one thing, they don't have emotions. But robots aren't simply machines or computers, either. Real robots are somewhere in between.

Robots are different from machines because a robot can be programmed to perform tasks. And robots are different from computers because they have moving parts. Roboticists often say a robot is a machine that can be programmed to perform a job and then reprogrammed to perform a different job. Most robots can move around and perform tasks without human help. But some robots, called telerobots, are remote controlled by humans, at least part of the time.

Robots do things that human beings do. They're especially good at jobs that are dull, dangerous, dirty or performed at a distance. They aren't bothered by extreme heat or cold, loud noise or toxic fumes — things that would cause problems for human workers. And robots never get careless or bored — or need a bathroom break!

*C-3PO (left) and R2-D2 (right)*

# Robot Roots

The word "robot" comes from the Czech word *robota*, which means forced work or drudgery. It was first used in 1921 by the writer Karel Capek in his play *R.U.R.* (short for Rossum's Universal Robots). In the play, the robots have emotions. They revolt, wipe out humans and start their own society.

In 1942, American scientist and writer Isaac Asimov wrote a story, "Runaround," that set out three laws of robot behavior:

Law 1: A robot may not injure a human being.

Law 2: A robot must obey orders given by human beings except when the orders conflict with the First Law.

Law 3: A robot must protect its own existence as long as this does not conflict with the First or Second Laws.

## Can a 'Bot Do It?

Humans can do all of these things. But can robots …
a. tie shoelaces?
b. play chess?
c. type on a keyboard?
d. play the piano?
e. dance?
f. use a paintbrush?
g. open a lock with a key

j. kick a soccer ball?
k. pick a coin off the floor?

Answers on page 47.

h. do a somersault
i. turn the pages of a book?

# ROBOTS UP CLOSE

All robots have the same basic parts, but they're put together in different ways, depending on the robot's ultimate use. Take a look at the parts on this imaginary robot.

## Brain

Most robots have computers for brains. The computer delivers precise instructions, telling the robot what to do and how. Computers are usually housed within the body of the robot. Some robots are remote controlled by humans, who provide the brains.

*Tiny silicon chips have made modern robotics possible. The chips hold huge amounts of information and enable computers to be super small, fast and powerful.*

## Power

A robot's power source supplies the energy the robot needs to operate. Robots usually get the power they need from batteries or solar panels. Some also generate power from the wind.

## Eyes, Ears, Nose and Skin

Cameras and sensors that sense heat, chemicals and light gather information for the robot. Many mobile robots use cameras to help them navigate and to find or avoid obstacles.

## Arm

Some robots are nothing but one big arm. Robots' arms are widely used in factories, in laboratories and on mobile robots. Robotic arms are similar to human arms — they have joints at the shoulder, elbow and wrist. The "end effector" (hand) can have different attachments, such as a welding torch or a water hose.

## Muscles

A motor connected to cables or gears moves wheels, legs or arms. Humanlike robots have dozens of small motors that each control movements in the face and neck, which make the robot more realistic.

## Put It All Together and You Get ...

Most robots have the same basic parts, but put together in different ways. So they often look different.

This panda robot has been designed to look kid-friendly for a reason — it's a toy. It uses sensors to interact with human play-mates. (For more on it, see page 35.)

NOMAD (below) looks more like a car than a robot.

It's been built to travel over ice and snow in Antarctica, using the sun and wind as its sources of power.

# ROBOTS AT WORK

Pick up a chocolate, put it in a box. Pick up a chocolate, put it in a box. Pick up a chocolate, put it in … Sigh! You get the idea.

Jobs in factories, even chocolate factories, can be boring and repetitive. Besides being dull, factory jobs can be dangerous, with huge, heavy, whirring machines, conveyor belts that never stop and welding torches throwing showers of sparks. Enter robots.

Most robots work in factories. They have replaced many human workers and work 24-7 assembling cars, appliances, electronics and toys. Robots also work in laboratories, paper mills and bottling plants. In fact, you will find robots anywhere they can lift, bolt, weld, sand, fold, stamp, wrap or paint, over and over (and over) again. Robots help factories churn out more products faster.

Most factory robots have large multijointed robotic arms that are programmed to do a specific task. If necessary, they can be reprogrammed and "re-tooled" to perform a different job. For example, a spray gun could be swapped for a drill.

Engineers plan how the robots will operate. They use 3-D computer modeling to plot out a robot's actions and move it safely around people in the factory. Then the engineers write a software program and download it into the robot's computerized "brain."

*Four-armed Adept Quattro (right) is a high-speed robot that's a packaging pro. It never gets bored and can put tiny items into packages hour after hour after hour without damaging or dropping a single one.*

*Robots are used for many jobs in car factories. The big orange arms you see below assemble, weld and paint car body parts. One car factory alone can have over 900 robots.*

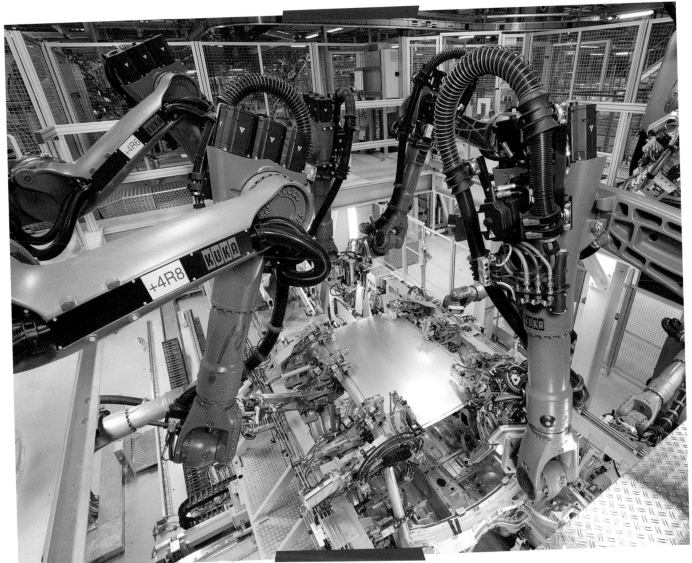

# HazBots: Robots In Danger Zones

It's a phone call no police department wants to get. Someone has planted a bomb on a train track. The area is evacuated, but the bomb still has to be located and defused. The bomb squad is alerted. Along with human bomb disposal experts, the team includes a robot. A human controller uses a video camera to direct the robot to find and defuse the bomb. Phew! The danger is over.

Robots are often used in situations that are too dangerous for people. Most often, these "hazbots" are remote controlled by a human operator. The robots gather information using a variety of sensors. They might use video cameras to survey the scene or even sensors that can "sniff" for hazardous chemicals, radiation or explosives. And some, like the bomb squad's Mini-Andros, actually put their "lives" on the line.

*Mini-Andros (below) is a bomb-defusing hazbot. It looks like a tiny tank and is small enough to fit in the trunk of a car.*

*Mini-Andros has three video cameras on its movable arms. The robot also has a microphone and a speaker, so it can "talk" (via its human operator) to any humans it might find.*

*Two movable tracks can be extended, so it can climb stairs and even cross small ditches. With tracks snugged in tight, Mini-Andros can maneuver in tight spaces.*

*Different tools can be added to Mini-Andros's arms so that it can break windows, see in the dark, blast water at a bomb or even pick up a bomb and place it in a bomb-proof box.*

## Reeking Robots

No human volunteers to find a problem in a sewer pipe? Send in MAKRO! It's not worried about keeping clean or smelling bad.

MAKRO follows a map of the sewer system stored in its computer brain. As it snakes through the pipes, it gathers information, including video, on the condition of the sewer. At 2 m (6.5 ft.) long, MAKRO is made of several segments and looks something like a caterpillar. Its shape helps it slink around tight corners and over ledges.

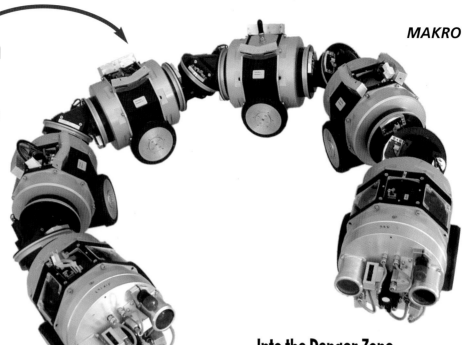

*MAKRO*

## Into the Danger Zone

In 1986, an accident at a nuclear power plant in Chernobyl, Ukraine, released radiation into the air, contaminating the area and making it unsafe for people.

If this disaster happened today, TALON might be sent in to survey the area. This rugged robot can withstand extreme heat and cold and even being submerged in water. It climbs stairs and rights itself if it tips over. Its sensors can test for dangerous gases, explosives, radiation and hazardous chemicals.

Robots like TALON enable humans to survey a scene before putting people in harm's way. The information these hazbots gather helps humans deal with environmental disasters.

*TALON*

## Robots to the Rescue

On the morning of September 11, 2001, two airplanes slammed into New York's World Trade Center, causing two office towers to collapse. When engineer Robin Murphy heard the news, she immediately wanted to help.

Murphy is the leader of the world's only robotic search-and-rescue team. She runs the Center for Robot Assisted Search and Rescue in Florida.

She knew that searching through the rubble might be dangerous for people and dogs. She also knew that her team of mini search-and-rescue robots could help.

Murphy sprang to action. She called her human team members, filled her van with mini-robots and drove nonstop from Florida to New York City.

The team arrived in the early morning of September 12, 2001. At the tense and highly emotional rescue scene, Murphy and her team had to talk authorities into letting them enter the disaster zone. When permission was finally granted, Murphy deployed her robots into the rubble. It was the first time robots were used for urban search and rescue.

Although the robots didn't find anyone alive, their 11-day search relayed a lot of valuable information to the human searchers. Murphy's team also demonstrated how humans and robots can work together to help survivors and searchers.

Robots are valuable members of a search-and-rescue team because they can go deeper into rubble than human searchers or rescue dogs can. Robots can also enter places you would never send a person — places in danger of collapsing, or filled with smoke, dust, water or dangerous chemicals.

*Robots were part of the search team at the collapse of the World Trade Center towers in New York on September 11, 2001.*

## Robot Heroes

At the World Trade Center, Murphy used the remote-controlled VGTV. This Canadian-designed robot is about the size of a shoe box. It acts as the eyes and ears of human rescuers. Microphones on the robot listen for sounds, such as human voices, and thermal cameras search for body heat.

*VGTV*

Tiny Microtrac robots were also deployed at the World Trade Center. These robots may be small — you can easily hold one in your hand — but they're tough. They travel on a rugged, single tread and are ideal for operating in tight spaces, including pipes and piles of rubble. Microtracs can be operated on land or under water.

*Microtrac*

Murphy used an iRobot PackBot in nearby buildings damaged when the World Trade towers fell. PackBots are small enough to fit in a backpack and can be transported easily and used in a variety of places, including battlefields. The heavy treads and tough construction of the PackBot make it perfect for rugged terrain. It can be tossed into a building, if necessary. If it flips over, a PackBot can right itself.

*iRobot PackBot*

# ROBOT, MD

There you are on the operating table. A doctor is about to give you an anesthetic that will send you to dreamland. Out of the corner of your eye, you see your surgeon on the other side of the room. His head is stuck in a viewing console and he's fiddling with the controls. Computer games in the operating room? Don't panic. This doctor is getting ready for surgery. His assistant? A four-armed robot.

From across the room, the doctor guides the robotic surgeon. In your drowsy stupor, you hear a whir and see a robotic arm move a tiny scalpel toward you. Another arm with a camera hovers nearby. Is this a dream? A science fiction movie? Nope, it's real. Robotic surgeons are starting to appear in operating rooms around the world.

One such robotic doctor is the da Vinci Surgical System, which you see here. With tiny surgical instruments attached to robotic arms and a high performance 3-D vision system, this robot can make precise movements that would be difficult for a human.

Operating with da Vinci or other robotic surgeons may be easier on the patient, too. Using a robotic system, incisions are tiny, only about the diameter of a pencil. Patients may lose less blood, have less pain and often get home to their own beds sooner.

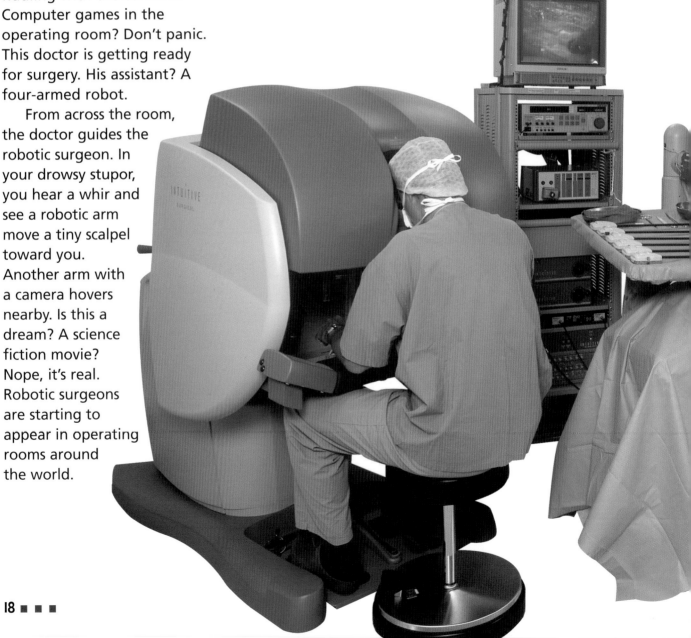

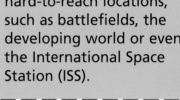

*The jointed "wrist" of da Vinci has a far greater range of motion than a human wrist has.*

## The Doctor Is Not In

In 2001, surgeons in New York used a remote-controlled robot to remove a woman's gallbladder ... 4800 km (3000 mi.) away in France. Using this new long-distance robotic technology, doctors can stay at home and assist in operations far away. That makes surgery possible for people in hard-to-reach locations, such as battlefields, the developing world or even the International Space Station (ISS).

## Gut 'Bots

Imagine having a robot roaming your insides. Scientists are experimenting with "nanobots," tiny robots with legs that may one day walk through parts of the human body, following directions from the doctor.

Using a camera, the robot would send the doctor pictures of the patient's insides. Who knows ... in the hospital of the future, you may swallow a tiny robot or have one injected through a needle to deliver medicines or clear blocked veins.

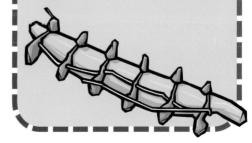

*The da Vinci Surgical System*

## Hospital Helpers

You're in a hospital elevator, clutching a box of chocolates for Aunt Rosie. When you reach your floor, an abandoned cart at the back of the elevator says, "Waiting to proceed." Startled, you move aside and watch the cart exit the elevator, roll down the hall, make a right turn and disappear out of sight.

You've just shared the elevator with TUG, a robotic courier used in hospitals to deliver medicines, food trays, X-rays, medical supplies, lab specimens and more. Using wireless radio signals, it can open doors and operate elevators. TUG communicates using flashing lights and can even say a few phrases, such as "Your deliveries are here."

TUG is just one of the types of robots being used in medical settings as assistants and even teachers. Here are a few more hospital helpers.

*TUG*

*Its two cameras help Penelope monitor its tools. This robot picks up tools using a magnetic "hand."*

## Pass the Scalpel, Please

Penelope (below) is a "scrub nurse" in an operating room. This robot can understand voice commands and delivers and retrieves instruments at the request of a surgeon. By taking care of the instruments, Penelope frees up human nurses to work directly with patients.

*Penelope (wrapped in plastic)*

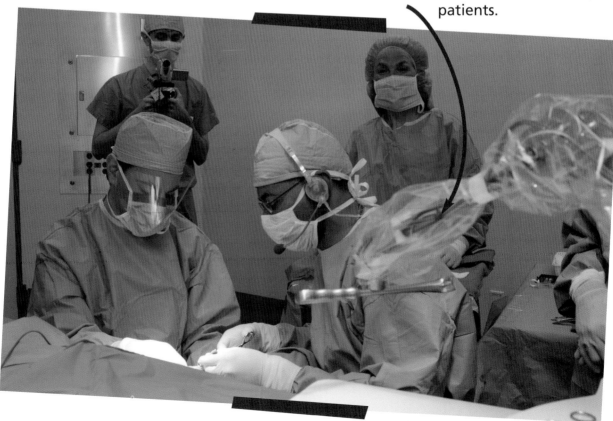

## Robo Mama

Noelle, the pregnant robot, teaches medical students how to help women give birth. She can be programmed to have different symptoms each time she delivers. She might have a long difficult labor one day and a quick unexpected birth the next. Noelle helps students develop their skills before they begin to work with real women and babies.

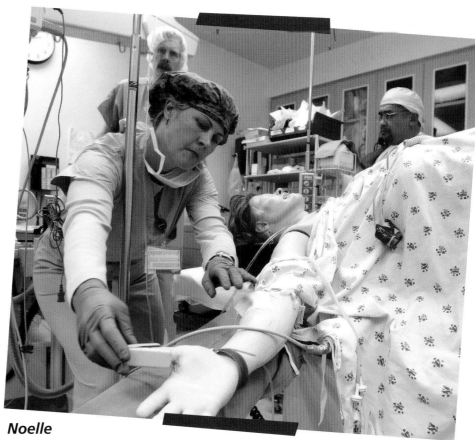

*Noelle*

## Bionic Body Bits

Claudia Mitchell lost her left arm in a motorcycle accident. Today, she has a robotic arm that she can control with her thoughts. When Mitchell thinks "close hand," that's exactly what happens.

Mitchell's robotic arm is a breakthrough. Until recently, people missing an arm or leg used prostheses (artificial arms or legs), which gave limited control and mobility. New robotic technologies are creating more lifelike replacements.

In Mitchell's case, doctors used nerves that had once linked her brain to her arm. They rerouted these nerves to her chest muscle. Now, when Claudia thinks "bend elbow," sensors in her robotic arm detect movement in her chest muscle and pass on the directions to a computer chip in the arm. The sensors then respond, and the robotic arm bends at the elbow. Six small motors control the arm.

Mitchell is able to pick up small objects, such as juice bottles, and can also detect heat and cold. The arm is still experimental and very expensive, but it is an important step in the creation of robotic limbs.

# ROBOT EXPLORERS

To investigate the extremes of Earth and beyond, explorers need to be willing to take risks. But some risks are just too great for human adventurers. That's when robots take over. They can boldly go where humans would like to, but can't.

Nothing scares robots — not the environmental extremes of distant planets, the molten lava of erupting volcanoes or the crushing pressure of the ocean's depths.

## Dive, Dive, Dive!

ROPOS is a robot submersible that's been on many undersea scientific expeditions. It takes video and photos, samples water temperature and chemistry and collects living things in its "bio box" and then delivers them to eager scientists on board the mother ship.

ROPOS is one of several remotely operated vehicles (ROVs) at work under the sea. Some lay and maintain submarine cables and pipelines; others keep an eye on oil platforms, collect samples and data for scientists, and help detect and remove potentially explosive underwater mines. ROVs are controlled by human operators at the surface who direct the submersibles' manipulator arms and tools.

*ROPOS*

## Doin' It Alone

SeaBED is an autonomous underwater vehicle (AUV) that can navigate on its own, controlled by onboard sensors and computers. It has mapped the seafloor and explored underwater hydrothermal vents, where boiling water bubbles up through the ocean floor.

Recently, SeaBED was used by its design team from Woods Hole Oceanographic Institution to search for shipwrecks in the Aegean Sea.

*SeaBED*

*SAUV II*

## Sun-powered Swimmer

Most AUVs are powered by batteries. When the batteries run out, so do they. But these AUVs are solarpowered, so they're called SAUVs. As long as there's sunlight, they can keep exploring. They store power in their batteries so they can work in the dark.

These AUVs are used to check for chemical and biological changes in lakes and rivers. One of their sensors can detect toxic chemicals and track the chemical trail to its source.

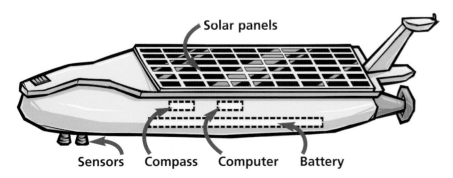

Solar panels

Sensors    Compass    Computer    Battery

# SPACE 'BOTS

Humans haven't made it past the Moon, and it's unlikely we will anytime soon. Space travel is just too dangerous. But not for robots. They can travel to faraway places where humans would be frozen, fried, crushed or poisoned.

The robot you see here is called Spirit. It and its twin, Opportunity, act as mobile Martian assistants for Earthling scientists. They've been exploring Mars since January 2004, taking photographs and analyzing soil and rock samples. One question they're helping to answer is whether there

was once liquid water on Mars. The rovers have found signs that there *was* water long ago. So there's a chance that Martians (well, tiny Martian microbes, at least) have lived on the Red Planet.

Scientists send the rovers instructions from Earth. Since there is a delay between the time a signal is sent and when it is received, the robots have to make some decisions on their own. For instance, the

human controller might instruct Spirit to travel to a certain rock, take a picture and transmit the image to Earth. As Spirit moves toward the rock, it uses its cameras and computer brain to figure out how to avoid obstacles. If it can't complete the job, Spirit alerts its controllers back on Earth and awaits further instruction.

Spirit and Opportunity have provided scientists with much more information than they ever dreamed of. These robotic rovers were expected to last only three months, but as of January 2008, they have been beaming back information for four years.

## Robonaut

Robonaut is a robot-astronaut that may one day work alongside human astronauts in space. Robonaut has highly sensitive arms, hands and fingers that can gather information on temperature, pressure and position. It will be operated by an astronaut inside the International Space Station (ISS) or back on Earth. The tele-operator wears a helmet and gloves wired to record his or her motions. This information is transferred to Robonaut, which then performs the same actions.

*Robonaut*

## Canadarm

The 17 m (56 ft.) long Canadarm2 is a giant robotic arm designed to help astronauts move cargo in space and to help with repair work on the ISS. The first Canadarm started traveling on space shuttles in 1981. Twenty years later, Canadarm2 was installed on the ISS. Next up? A two-armed robot, Dextre, capable of using smaller, more precise tools.

*Canadarm2*

# In Our Image: The Droids

In the regal dining room of a palace in Prague, Czech Republic, a child-sized robot greets the Czech prime minister and shakes his hand.

The Japanese prime minister had brought an unusual date to this diplomatic dinner — the robot ASIMO.

ASIMO, or **A**dvanced **S**tep in **I**nnovative **MO**bility, is one of the world's most advanced humanoid, or humanlike, robots. It can walk (forward, backward and sideways), climb stairs, run, open doors, carry light objects and, yes, even balance on one foot while kicking a soccer ball.

ASIMO's eyes are cameras, which allows it to navigate and even recognize people. (And, if these people are stored in its database, ASIMO will address them by name!)

ASIMO was designed by Honda. They've already put this pint-sized 'bot to work as a goodwill ambassador. It also welcomes visitors at one of the company's offices, shows people to meeting rooms and can deliver a trolley of mail or sandwiches.

It took over 20 years for Honda scientists to develop ASIMO. It was the first robot to walk smoothly, in a humanlike way. Its fluid motion is controlled by 34 motors.

ASIMO is battery-powered and needs recharging after about one hour. The battery is housed in its body. The powerful computers needed to direct ASIMO's movement are in its backpack.

ASIMO and other humanoid robots are being designed to help people, both at work and in the home. In the future, these robots may be receptionists, security guards, entertainers, delivery 'bots, tourist guides and cleaners. In fact, some of them are already doing these jobs.

# The Leg Lab

It must be easier to design a robot with two legs than one with six or eight legs, right? Nope. Creating a robot that walks on just two legs is an enormous challenge. Think of how you walk. Every time you lift your leg to move, you shift your weight to the other leg. Back and forth, back and forth, your weight shifts with each step. A robot has to do the same thing.

To design a robot that can walk, roboticists first study human anatomy and watch how people's muscles, bones and joints work together. Then they take this information and translate it into a computer program.

Many researchers specialize in trying to figure out how robots move. They experiment with different designs to find those that are the most stable and practical. Here are some of their walking, hopping and swimming wonders.

## Uniroo

*Uniroo was the first robot to jump like a kangaroo. It has three joints in its leg, which act like your hip, knee and ankle joints. Uniroo also has a small tail.*

*Denise*

## Denise

*Denise might have a bucket for a head, but she walks like a human. Her swinging arms and flexible knees and ankles give her a very humanlike stride.*

## Amphibot

*Part eel, part salamander, all robot. Amphibot can swim by "snaking" its body back and forth. Then, when the robot hits the shore, its four legs take over.*

*Amphibot*

*Uniroo*

# BEAUTY AND THE 'BOT

Look closely at the woman below. Is she real or is she a robot? Meet Repliee, one of the most humanlike robots created to date. Unlike ASIMO, who is a humanoid (a robot that looks a bit like a human), Repliee is an android (a robot made to look identical to a human).

*Professor Ishiguro and his robot*

*Repliee*

A good wig, nice clothes and realistic "skin" (made by taking a silicon mold of a real person's face) all help. And 42 mechanical devices, called actuators, create a variety of facial expressions and other body movements that add to the illusion.

Repliee has been designed to move its upper body in a smooth, natural fashion. It can't walk, but using cameras, microphones and other sensors, it can tell when humans are near and talk to them.

Repliee's creators think that we can learn about human behavior by making robots like Repliee. For the most part, Repliee is just for show. It has worked as a "greeter" at robot expositions, and its designers think it would make a great museum guide or company "spokesperson."

## Brother 'Bot

Which is Dr. Hiroshi Ishiguro and which is his "twin," Geminoid? Ishiguro's twin is a robot that works like a very complicated puppet. Ishiguro can control Geminoid using a computer and even operate him remotely. Geminoid mimics Ishiguro's movements, posture and speech. Ishiguro says that one day he might use Geminoid to help him do part of his job as a university professor. Professor Ishiguro's students might be surprised to see Geminoid delivering a lecture in his place!

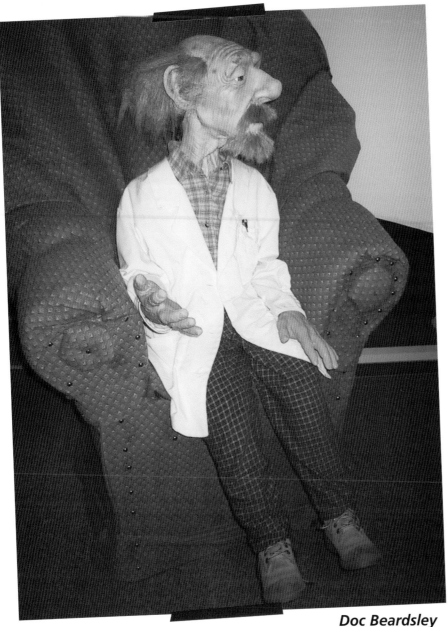

*Doc Beardsley*

But Doc is different from most animatronic figures. He can see and hear, understand speech and carry on a conversation. When you speak to him, he will follow your face with his eyes.

Doc's inventors are interested in seeing how people react to robots. They are working hard to make Doc as lifelike as possible. That's not easy. Humans make all sorts of small movements, such as blinks and twitches, that make them … well, more human.

Recently, Doc got a "facelift." His metal, plastic and fake fur face was covered with a smooth silicon skin, which you see here. His creators are also trying to program his movements to be more natural.

As technology improves, it might become more difficult to tell which is a 'bot and which is not!

## What's Up Doc?

Horatio "Doc" Beardsley looks and acts like an absentminded professor. He entertains all who will listen with stories (he claims his parents were Austrian goat herders) and inventions (such as the foon, a cross between a fork and a spoon). Sometimes, he even burps and hiccups. Doc is an animatronic character invented by roboticists in Pittsburgh, Pennsylvania.

Animatronic characters are lifelike models with preset moves and prerecorded sounds. They are often used in theme parks or museums.

# ROBOTS AT HOME

Too tired to mow the lawn, vacuum the living room or wash the kitchen floor? No worries, a robot can do it for you. These are a few of the household robots making their way into our homes and gardens.

*Drop this robot into the pool and it uses a water jet and vacuum to clean away the grime while you sip another drink poolside.*

*IRobot Roomba vacuums a room with the help of sensors that tell it when it's too close to a wall or other obstacles.*

*This guard 'bot monitors a home to detect movement and can contact its owner or sound an alarm if it detects intruders or smells smoke or gas. When its power runs low, the robot finds its charger and plugs itself in.*

*Robotic lawn mowers mow your lawn and not the neighbor's by staying in an area defined by a wire buried around the lawn's edge.*

*The iRobot Scooba sweeps, washes, scrubs and dries your floor. Scooba, dooba, doo!*

*Wakamaru helps care for the elderly by reminding them to take their medications. Its camera "eyes" can also send video images to doctors or family members. Wakamaru also acts as a security guard, alerting its owners to intruders.*

WELCOME HOME

All of these robots work in areas that are fairly flat. It's harder to design robots for 3-D spaces. So it may be a long time before there are robots that make your bed or take out the garbage. For now at least, you'll have to keep those chores on your to-do list.

# ROBOT FUN & GAMES

Not all robots are hard at work in factories and laboratories, battlefields and outer space. Some are out there wrestling, playing soccer and even racing camels. A few are winning medals at RoboGames, a robot version of the Olympic Games.

RoboGames is the highlight of the year for robot enthusiasts. Amateur robot builders from all over the world enter their creations in over 70 competitions, including gymnastics (where 'bots perform somersaults and cartwheels), stair climbing, dancing, soccer and much more.

**Robo soccer is the most popular robotic sport. Teams chase a ball on a "field" the size of a Ping-Pong table.**

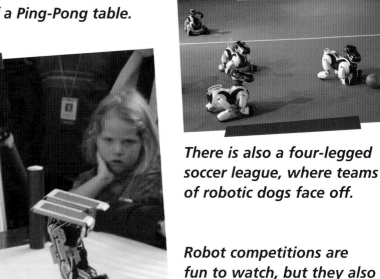

**There is also a four-legged soccer league, where teams of robotic dogs face off.**

**Robot competitions are fun to watch, but they also have a serious side. The work of robot keeners helps push the boundaries of what robots can do. The competitions help develop new technologies and also refine the skills of future roboticists.**

*Many young people build their first robot using a LEGO Mindstorms robotic kit. Competitions at the RoboGames and LEGO Leagues give these keen 'bot builders a chance to show off their designs.*

# Robo Riders

In Qatar and the United Arab Emirates, robots are making the lives of children safer.

In these countries, children as young as four have been kidnapped or sold by their families to work as lightweight jockeys in camel races.

Enter Kamel. This camel-riding robot is replacing young kids as camel jockeys.

# ROBOTIC PALS

Looking for a pet that doesn't need to be fed, groomed or have its poop scooped? Try a robopet!

## Meet Pleo

Pleo looks like a one-week-old Camarasaurus, a dinosaur from the Jurassic period, but that's where the resemblance ends. Unlike the real Camarasaurus, Pleo uses 38 sensors to detect light, motion, touch and sound.

It has two microprocessors that can make 60 million calculations per second.

Processing information from its sensors, Pleo can respond in many ways. A light sensor in its nose tells this robopet whether it's bright or dark. If it's dark and Pleo thinks it's bedtime, it might curl up and go to sleep. Sensors in its head, back and legs tell Pleo when it is being touched. It can crane its head around to see who's scratching its back.

As Pleo interacts with its owner and environment, it changes its behavior. Like a real pet, it learns new behaviors when it is rewarded. Treat Pleo kindly and you'll have a mellow, pleasant pet. But neglect it at your peril. Ignore Pleo and it sulks.

*Pleo*

*Robopanda*

## Panda Pal

Robopanda is a plastic playmate with a difference. It's a robotic friend that will tell you stories, play games, sing songs and even crack a joke or two.

In its "training mode," Robopanda teaches its owner how to play with it. For instance, it might instruct you to "Touch my head for games." Once it gets to know you more, it might greet you with "Let's play a game" when you walk into the room.

Robopanda can crawl on all fours, then get back up into a sitting position. If you aren't around to play with Robopanda, it has its own friend — a stuffed panda. Robopanda plays with its buddy, chatting to it and giving it a cuddle.

*NeCoRo*

## Pet Therapy

Cats, dogs and other pets are often used to comfort people who are ill or sad. But pets are not allowed in many hospitals, schools or nursing homes. Robotic pets can help fill the desire for a furry friend.

NeCoRo, a cuddly robotic cat, has touch sensors in its back, chin and head. As it is held and petted, it responds by purring. NeCoRo can't walk, but it can sit, stretch and wag its tail.

*Two Paros cuddle*

Paro is modeled after a baby harp seal and, from a distance, it would be hard to tell from the real thing. Paro is sensitive to touch, light, sound and temperature. When stroked, it moves its head and flippers, blinks its eyes and makes cooing sounds. It can also recognize its name and the voices of certain people.

# The Robotic Future

*Stanley*

Here's a challenge for you. Design a car capable of racing 210 km (130 mi.) across the rugged Mojave Desert, through potholes and dried-up riverbeds, around boulders and other obstacles. Oh, but there's one thing — no driver allowed.

In 2004, 15 teams of keen roboticists accepted the challenge and created autonomous (self-driving) vehicles, outfitted with a variety of cameras, lasers and sensors, a GPS (global positioning system) and computer software. Not one of the robotic vehicles finished — they all either crashed, burned or stalled.

But a year later, a blue Volkswagen SUV named Stanley (shown on page 36) completed the race in 6 hours, 54 minutes. Hot on Stanley's heels … er, wheels, were four other vehicles that also made it to the finish line. In just one year, adjustments to vehicle and sensor designs and improved software programs made all the difference.

Things can change quickly in the world of robots. New technologies and innovations, such as smaller, faster and cheaper computer chips or improvements in robotic sensors and moveable joints, can make a big difference to what roboticists can create.

Stanley's success came from the computer program that "drove" the car. Instead of writing a program with endless instructions, Stanley's designers used a system of "machine learning." In the weeks before the race, a human driver sat in Stanley and drove. A computer monitored the driving and "learned" from it.

Computers learning? Robots that are smart? One of the rowdiest debates among roboticists today is just how intelligent robots are or might become. Are robots only as smart as the humans who make them … or can they be smarter?

## How Intelligent Are Robots?

On May 11, 1997, a computer called Deep Blue forced the reigning world chess champion Garry Kasparov to withdraw from a chess game he knew he would lose. The computer won.

Deep Blue was "smart" — after all, it could consider 400 million chess moves per second. But was Deep Blue intelligent? Although Deep Blue could play chess, it couldn't play a round of Go Fish, nor could it answer a simple question such as "Is the sky blue?"

Robots are programmed to perform a specific task or set of tasks. A roboticist writes a computer program that makes it possible. Most of today's robots just mimic intelligence by drawing on this program or other stored information. But many roboticists think we need to look at robotic intelligence differently. And they're looking to the human brain for ideas.

# MIND OVER METAL

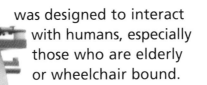

People often imagine robots like those that star in cartoons — cheerful household helpers whizzing around the home doing our chores. A robot like this is a long way off, but Domo brings us one step closer. This robot was designed to interact with humans, especially those who are elderly or wheelchair bound.

*Domo*

Domo is a robotic helper that can work with humans to do household tasks such as putting away dishes. Up to now, this task, which is so simple for humans, was not practical for robots. Roboticists would have to anticipate every possible item that could be found in a kitchen and program the robot to grasp and store it. This was time consuming for the roboticist and for the robot, which would have to sort through all the possible options in its database with every action. And the robot could only deal with something a human had programmed into its computer brain. Throw in a new spatula and the robot couldn't cope.

Domo's inventors tried something new. In addition to giving Domo a program with instructions on how to recognize and handle kitchen objects, they also gave Domo unprogrammed "nerve cells" and a body riddled with sensitive touch sensors. If the robot is presented an object

## No Brainer

BEAM robots don't rely on a computer brain. Instead, they use simple sensors and circuits (much like the circuits in a radio) to perform tasks, such as moving toward a light or avoiding obstacles.

Since these robots are made using basic parts and don't have complicated computer programs, they are a popular robot to build at home. BEAM robots are often fuelled by solar power.

it doesn't recognize, such as a new spatula, information from sensors feeds the robot's nerve network. The robot stores the information it gathers so the next time it will react appropriately. Over time, the robot continuously adds new information to its database, but it also draws on what it has stored from previous experience, much like humans do. Domo is a robot that can learn.

Brainy new 'bots like Domo are expanding our ideas of how humans and robots might one day live and work together.

# BRinGinG UP BAByBOT

Cynthia Breazeal enters her lab and finds her robot, Kismet, dozing on the desk. Breazeal sits in front of Kismet, wiggles her hand to say hello and slowly moves her head back and forth. The robot seems to wake up. Kismet opens its big, blue eyes and lifts its pink ears. Soon, Kismet looks excited and breaks into a big smile. It's hard not to smile too, watching scientist and robot interact like a mother and child.

This is exactly the interaction that Breazeal wants to mimic. Breazeal sees herself in the role of a parent, while Kismet is a child. Just like a baby, Kismet learns as it interacts with Breazeal. For instance, it has learned how to interpret body language and other clues that tell how someone is feeling. Kismet uses a range of sensors and 16 small computers working together to learn. As it "grows," Kismet can build on skills and information previously learned.

Breazeal deliberately gave Kismet an appealing face, with furry eyebrows, big eyes, ears that can wiggle and red metal lips. She thinks that people want to interact with something that looks human. Plus, humans know how to read the emotions of a human, or humanlike, face. From experience, humans know when another person is happy, sad, angry or bored.

Just like in a human relationship, Breazeal and Kismet respond to one another. When Kismet shows

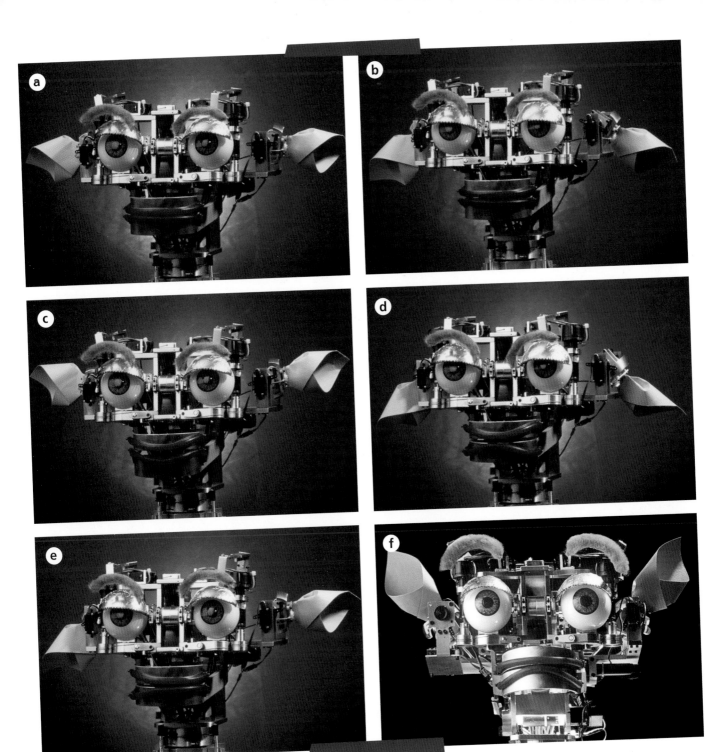

it's bored, Breazeal might play with the robot by wiggling a stuffed toy in front of its face. In turn, Kismet responds by perking up, smiling and looking excited. But if Breazeal overdoes it and wiggles the toy too fast, too close or for too long, Kismet responds by looking annoyed or even scared.

Breazeal designed Kismet to study how humans and humanoid robots interact over time. At first, Kismet was quite helpless, like a newborn baby. But as Breazeal worked with the robot, it acquired new skills and slowly added to its store of information, just like a human baby does.

*Kismet's face is very expressive and shows a range of emotions. From the top left, the emotions shown here are: a) calmness, b) tiredness, c) happiness, d) anger, e) disgust and f) fear.*

# SwaRm 'BoTs

Today's smartest robots are about as intelligent as ants, but real ants are no dummies. Ants are industrious, successful animals that work together in teams. Some roboticists were inspired by

the idea of teams and have created swarms of small robots that share information and work together.

In the future, robot swarms may be used in danger zones or in areas that are just too large for a single robot. Take Mars, for example. It's both dangerous and big. Dozens of robots could fan out over Mars's surface. As they explored, they could communicate with one another, sharing data and using the information to make group decisions. And there's an added bonus: more robots means that more information could be collected and beamed back to Earth.

*This team of 100 Centibots is checking out a hallway. As they travel, the robots gather and share information with one another and with a central command center. One day, similar robot teams could explore and map danger zones, such as buildings full of smoke or gas. Teams might have different skills. For instance, the first team might be programmed to create a map of the danger area, with each robot mapping a different section. The second team could use this map to search the area, relaying information back to the human team stationed outside the danger zone.*

## A 'Bot in the Hand

In 1992, James McLurkin built one of the world's smallest robots. Called Goliath, it fit on the palm of McLurkin's hand with lots of room to spare.

McLurkin is interested in using swarms of tiny robots to perform big tasks. To get ideas, he's studied swarms of ants.

McLurkin's robots are simple, small and don't have a lot of computer memory. They don't have a human directing their behavior, either. Instead, the robots communicate with one another and share information to get their job done.

McLurkin's work is still experimental, but he can get his swarms to perform a variety of tasks such as follow, cluster together, surround, navigate and even play music. It's up to the robots to figure out how to complete their task as a team.

# COOL OR CREEPY?

People and animals with robotic parts? They are called cyborgs, short for cybernetic organisms. That means they're a mix of natural and artificial. People who create cyborgs think that adding technology can give living things greater abilities.

Cyborgs might sound futuristic but, if so, the future is here. Scientists are already starting to add robotic bits to living things.

## Robo-roaches

In one experiment, Japanese scientists have given cockroaches robotic parts by replacing their antennae with electrodes. They've also given the roaches little backpacks with cameras and microphones.

The scientists can remotely stimulate the electrodes, which control the cockroaches' movements, turning them into tiny, living robots. They think their robo-roaches could be used to search through the rubble of collapsed buildings, but the roaches would also make mighty sneaky, and creepy, spies.

## Robo-rodents

In another experiment in the U.S., electrodes were implanted into the brains of five rats so humans could dictate the rats' movements. The scientists remote controlled the rats to run, turn, jump and climb.

Could robot rats be used in disasters where people might be buried? Maybe. But using live animals for such experiments is controversial and, some say, unethical.

Robotic roaches and rats? What's next? Robotic people? Read on …

GOT ROBO-ROACHES? GOT ROBO-RODENTS?

GET ROBO-EXTERMINATOR!

*Kevin Warwick*

## A Cyborg Named Kevin

How close will people and robots come? What if people were part robot? English scientist Kevin Warwick is experimenting with this idea.

In 1988, he had a silicon chip implanted in his arm. For several months, computers in Warwick's office building monitored his movements, and the chip relayed signals that automatically opened doors and turned on lights, computers and other electronic equipment.

A second, more complex implant was linked directly to the nerves of Warwick's left arm in 2002. This device sent signals from his nervous system to a computer. The data from this experiment was used to design a robotic arm.

Warwick considers himself a cyborg. His ideas are experimental, but he is examining the idea of how robots might become more than just household helpers or factory workers. In the future, will humans get more robotic or will robots get more human? Can robots make humans "better," allowing us to do things we normally could not? Stay tuned.

## Definitely Cool

If you think mixing humans and robots is creepy, we've got news for you. Adding or implanting mechanical parts to human bodies can be extremely cool. It's also extremely current.

Pacemakers are implanted into chests to keep heartbeats regular. They monitor the natural electrical signals of a heart and, when necessary, send impulses that correct the heart's rhythm.

Cochlear implants in human ears help with hearing. A microphone in the implant picks up sounds from the environment. The sounds are then translated into electrical impulses, which are sent to the brain.

And prostheses (artificial limbs), like Claudia Mitchell's bionic arm on page 21, help amputees regain abilities they have lost.

Does this make these people cyborgs? Maybe. But if so, it's a good thing. Their robotic parts may not have given them bionic or superhuman abilities, but they have helped restore a healthy level of function in their ears, heart or limbs.

# INTO THE FUTURE

 In the 1970s, there were no laptops, iPods or BlackBerries. Computers were large and cumbersome and certainly not something everyone had in their home. Nor could most people even imagine needing a computer. What would they use it for?

Fast forward to today, where most homes and all workplaces regularly use computers. Can you imagine the world without computers or the Internet? The creation of common programming languages and smaller, faster and less expensive computer components has quickly changed the way we communicate with one another and carry out our day-to-day lives. We are living in a Computer Age.

Today, in thousands of labs around the world, as well as in many homes and schools, people are tinkering with robots. Some are building their own robots just for fun. Others are trying to perfect robotic sensors or figure out new ways for robots to learn through experience. Yet right now, most of us can't imagine why we would use or need a robot. They sound like fun, and it would be nice to have a robot to do tedious chores, but are they really necessary?

Does this thinking sound familiar? Perhaps we are with robots today where we were with computers in the 1970s — on the cusp of something BIG. Is the Robotic Age just around the corner?

# GLOSSARY

**3-D:** Three-dimensional, having height, width and depth.

**anatomy:** The structure of animals and their parts.

**androids:** Robots made to look identical to humans.

**animatronic figures:** Lifelike models with preset moves and prerecorded sounds. Often used in amusement parks or museums.

**autonomous underwater vehicles (AUVs):** Robots that can navigate underwater on their own, controlled by onboard sensors and computers.

**circuit:** A complete pathway or loop for the flow of electricity.

**cyborgs:** Cybernetic organisms. Animals, including humans, with robotic parts.

**database:** An organized collection of information stored in a computer.

**humanoids:** Humanlike robots.

**laser:** A device that produces a very concentrated beam of light.

**microbes:** Very small organisms that can only be seen using a microscope.

**program:** A series of instructions for a computer.

**prostheses:** Artificial body parts, usually arms or legs.

**radiation:** Energy that is transmitted in the form of waves or particles. Overexposure to radiation can be dangerous to living things.

**remote controlled:** Operated from a distance.

**remotely-operated vehicles (ROVs):** Vehicles, such as submarines or cars, that are operated from a distance.

**robots:** Machines that can be programmed to perform a job and then reprogrammed to perform a different job.

**roboticists:** People who design and/or build robots.

**sensors:** Devices that can sense things, such as heat, light, sound or the presence of certain gases.

**submersibles:** Diving vessels that can operate under water.

**telerobots:** Robots controlled from a distance (remote controlled) by humans.

---

# ANSWERS

## *Can a 'Bot Do It?*, page 9
Although not all robots are able to do all of these things, there are robots that can play chess, play the piano, dance, use a paintbrush, do a somersault and kick a soccer ball.

# INDEX